BEAUTIFUL ZOO ANIMALS

TO COME AND SEE!

This book belongs to:

....

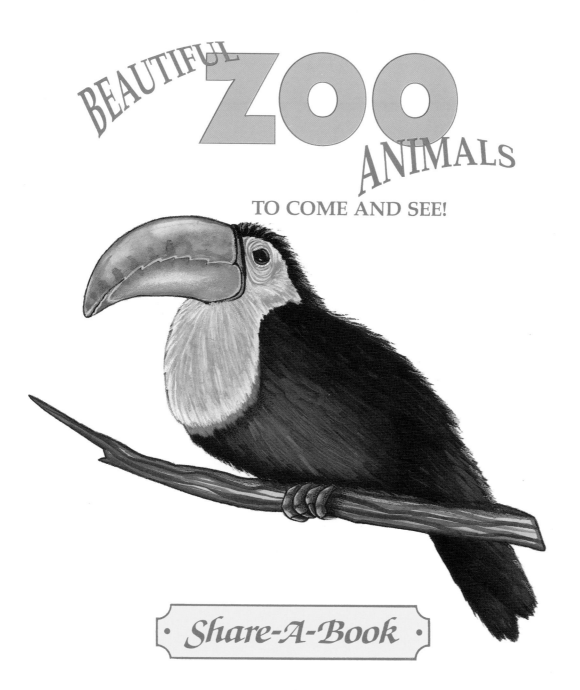

BEAUTIFUL ZOO ANIMALS

TO COME AND SEE!

· Share-A-Book ·

Polar bears are independent and usually like to hunt and wander alone. They can grow up to ten feet tall and weigh as much as 1,000 pounds.

Elephants are usually peaceful animals known by their enormous size, large ears, and long nose, called a trunk.

Zebras are wild horses that live in Africa. They can be recognized by their vivid stripes.

The male lion proudly displays a beautiful mane and is often called the "King of Beasts." Lions live in a family group called a pride.

The rhinoceros lives in herds in Africa.
They have large horns on their noses and
can weigh up to two tons.

Giraffes are the
tallest animals in
the world. With
their long necks,
they feed on the
leaves high up
in the tops of
trees.

The kangaroo is a marsupial, or pouched animal. A baby kangaroo is called a "joey" and spends most of its time in its mother's pouch.

Tigers can live in many different climates and are excellent swimmers. Their stripes help to camouflage them in the brush so they can hunt their prey without being seen.

Sea lions spend their time swimming and eating fish. They make a loud noise that sounds like barking.

Toucans have large, colorful beaks they use for feeding on fruit and insects. Although they may look awkward, their beaks are actually very light and strong.

The spots in a leopard's coat are called "rosettes." Even black leopards, called panthers, have subtle spots in their beautiful coats.

Pandas will rest during the day and feed at night on bamboo shoots.

The hippopotamus will spend his days floating in the water to stay cool. At night, he will come out to feed on grass and plants.

Camels with two humps like a dry climate and they drink very little water. They have thick, shaggy coats that help to keep them warm.

Walruses live in the icy
region near the North Pole.
They use their large tusks
to scrape food from the
ocean floor.

**Look for other
titles in this series:**

Friendly Farm Animals
Furry Wild Animals
Incredible Dinosaurs